shibori

the art of indigo dyeing

with step-by-step techniques and 25 projects to make

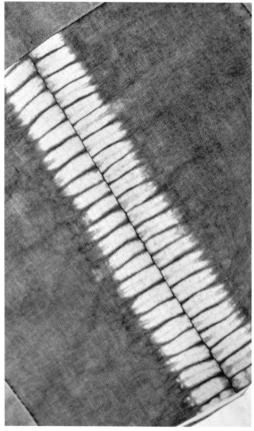

Nicola Gouldsmith

CICO BOOKS

LONDON NEW YORK

This book is dedicated to my son
Miles Gouldsmith, a great inspiration!

This edition published in 2018 by CICO Books
An imprint of Ryland Peters & Small Ltd

20–21 Jockey's Fields   341 E 116th St
London WC1R 4BW   New York, NY 10029

www.rylandpeters.com

10 9 8 7 6 5 4 3 2 1

Parts of this book were first published in 2014 under the title *Indigo*.

A CIP catalog record for this book is available from the Library of
Congress and the British Library.

ISBN: 978 1 78249 598 7

Printed in China

Editor: Clare Sayer
Design concept: Vicky Rankin
Photographer: Gavin Kingcome
Stylists: Nel Haynes and Jo Thornhill
Illustrator: Harriet de Winton

Art director: Sally Powell
Production manager: Gordana Simacovic
Publishing manager: Penny Craig
Publisher: Cindy Richards

Notes

For most of the projects you will need a **basic sewing kit** of scissors,
needles, pins, tape measure, and sewing thread.

CICO Books have made every effort to provide safe and accurate
instructions for the projects in this book. However, the publisher cannot
accept liability for injuries or property damage that might occur from
attempting to make the projects.

Always take care when handling dye and other chemicals, and keep
them out of reach of children and animals.

Contents

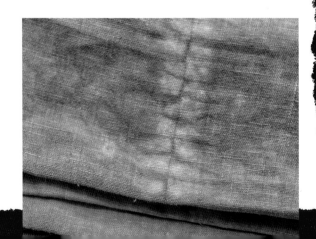

Introduction

Indigo is the most commonly used dye in shibori. It is extracted from the leaves of the plant *Indigofera tinctoria*, and has been used for centuries to dye all kinds of fabric a rich, vibrant blue. From its origins as a naturally produced dye, most common in India, to its ubiquitous appearance in blue jeans today, indigo has traveled far and wide.

Dyeing with indigo

Indigo extract is available in the form of a powder that is easily obtained from craft and dye stores, some of which are listed on page 118.

During the dyeing process indigo powder is used along with the minerals spectralite and soda ash, also available from craft and dye stores. These chemicals should all be used with care, and stored away from and out of reach of children and pets. Be sure to wear rubber gloves when using these materials, and wash your hands after handling them.

Spectralite removes the oxygen present in water. Once the oxygen is no longer present, the indigo powder will dissolve. We then add a soda ash solution in small amounts at a time in order to alter the pH level. The soda ash raises the pH: to dye animal fibers like wool or silk we need it to be ph9; for plant fibers such as cotton or linen we need it to be ph11.

Use only old utensils and pots that will never be used for food preparation again. And as indigo is very strong, keep the pan you use just for indigo, do not use it for other dyes.

Indigo dyeing is also quite messy so you will need an apron and it is best to dye outside if possible. Along with the usual warnings about using dyes, there is one other: beware, indigo dyeing is addictive!

Indigo dyeing requires the use of two vats or containers, one large and one smaller. The smaller one is used for the preparation of the indigo solution; a large glass jar with a lid is ideal for this, as you can see what is going on and keep the solution covered. The larger vat is the one you will actually dip your fabrics into, and a large old saucepan is useful for this.

As you dye with indigo, it is very important to avoid introducing oxygen into the dye vat. It is possible to minimize this by sliding the fabric carefully down one side of the vat without disturbing the surface. Where an even finish is required, the fibers can be "worked" under the surface with your fingers for a few moments. When removing the fabric from the vat, leave a tail of fabric in the vat through which excess dye can dribble back into the vat. This is also done at the side of the vat, to prevent splashing which would introduce oxygen into the vat.

Once you have finished dyeing, there are a few things to remember about storing dye solutions. Soda ash solution can be stored in plastic bottles for future use. Label well and store away from pets and children. An indigo vat that still has dye present can also be covered and saved to be revived at a later date. It can be revived by adding a teaspoonful of spectralite and warming; after an hour, a blue metallic layer will be on the surface and it will be ready to use.

A safe and fun way to dispose of a used vat is to add shredded newspaper to the liquid until it is all soaked up, and then use the paper pulp for sculpting or paper-making.

Preparing the indigo vat

You will need

- 1 oz (25 g) indigo powder— this will dye 4½ lb (2 kg) of fiber or fabric
- Spectralite
- 1¼ pt (600 ml) warm water
- Large glass jar with a screw-top lid
- Teaspoon
- 5¼ oz (150 g) soda ash
- Jug
- Litmus paper (to test pH level)
- Large pan with a lid

1 Place the indigo powder in the glass jar with 3 teaspoons (15 ml) of spectralite and a little of the warm water. Stir well to make a paste, then mix in ½ pt (200 ml) of the warm water.

2 Add the soda ash to the rest of the warm water in a jug and stir well. Add the soda ash solution to the indigo solution a little at a time, using the litmus paper to check the pH level after each addition. Stop adding the soda solution when the desired pH is reached (see the note on fibers on page 7).

3 Cover the jar by placing the lid on loosely, and set it aside in a warm place for the solution to develop (it must be kept warm for this to happen). This will take 30–40 minutes. While this is happening, prepare the large vat by filling a large pan two-thirds full with warm water and adding 1 tsp (5 ml) of spectralite to it. Keep this pan covered and warm.

4 The indigo solution in the jar is ready when you can see both a metallic blue layer on the surface and a yellow liquid beneath. This is due to the dye on the surface of the vat reacting with oxygen in the air; the liquid below remains yellow because it is not in contact with any oxygen.

5 Add the indigo solution to the spectralite solution in the large vat by lowering the jar into the vat; do not pour the indigo solution in, as pouring could cause splashing, which would introduce oxygen into the vat.

6 Leave the vat covered and warm for an hour. It is ready to use when the surface of the vat is covered in metallic blue bubbles with an oily appearance.

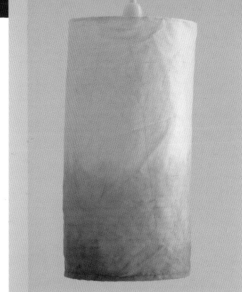

chapter 1

Plain and Dip-Dyeing

If you are new to dyeing, then plain dyeing (simply dyeing a whole piece of fabric) will help you master the technique of preparing the indigo vat, and become familiar with the effect of the dye on different fabrics. Dip-dyeing, where only part of the fabric is dipped into the vat, with less being dipped each time, is another simple technique for beginners to try.

plain and dip-dyeing Techniques

Plain dyeing is, by its nature, the most straightforward technique. The fabric is immersed in a prepared indigo vat for just a few seconds, then rinsed several times, washed, and dried to produce a piece of plain blue fabric. Dip-dyeing produces different results, as you can vary the shade of indigo by building up layers, airing, and allowing the dye to develop each time before repeating the dipping process. Because items only need to be dipped into the indigo vat for a few moments, an attractive graded effect can be achieved easily and quickly, with the color ranging from light blue to darkest indigo.

You will need
- Fabric
- Prepared indigo vat (see page 8)
- Rubber gloves and apron
- Bowls for soaking and rinsing
- White household vinegar
- Washing detergent

To plain dye

1 Soak the fabric in clean, cold water for a couple of hours to prevent air pockets forming. (If oxygen is present, the dye won't work.) Remove from the bowl and gently squeeze out all the excess water.

2 Immerse all of the fabric in the dye vat for a few seconds, taking care to disturb the surface of the dye solution as little as possible by sliding the fabric in down the side of the vat. Work the fibers under the surface with your fingers in order to get an even result.

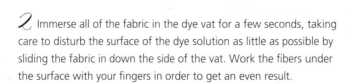

3 Remove the fabric from the solution slowly, at the side of the vat, leaving a tail of fabric in the vat through which excess dye can dribble gently back into it. Air the fabric to develop the color—this can happen very quickly! You can either hold the fabric or, for larger pieces, drape them over a washing line. It is best to do this outdoors, because dye solution will drip from the fabric. If you want a darker shade, dip the fabric in the vat again for a few seconds, as above, and air the fabric again. Continue to dip and air until you are happy with the shade.

4 Rinse the fabric in several changes of cold water, until dye no longer comes out of the fabric. Rinse once more, adding white household vinegar to the final rinse. You will need about ¼ pt (100 ml) of vinegar per 2 pt (1 l) of water in the final rinse. This neutralizes the pH, to prevent damage to the fabric. Wash with detergent and hang the fabric out to dry.

To dip dye

1 Soak the fabric in clean, cold water for a couple of hours to prevent air pockets from forming. (If oxygen is present, the dye won't work.) Remove from the bowl and gently squeeze out all the excess water.

2 Dip a portion of the fabric into the dye vat, aiming to disturb the surface as little as possible by sliding the fabric in down the side of the vat. This first portion will be the total extent of the dip-dyed area. Work the fibers under the surface with your fingers in order to get an even result.

3 Remove the fabric from the solution slowly at the side of the vat, leaving a tail of fabric in the vat through which excess dye can dribble gently back into it. Air the fabric to develop the color, either by holding the fabric or, for larger pieces, by draping them over a washing line. It is best to do this outdoors, because dye solution will drip from the fabric.

4 Repeat the dipping process several times, leaving a little more of the fabric out of the vat each time. This way a gradual darkening effect can be achieved, with the end of the fabric that is dipped most often being the darkest blue.

5 Rinse the fabric in several changes of cold water, until dye no longer comes out of the fabric. Rinse once more, adding white household vinegar to the final rinse. You will need about ¼ pt (100 ml) of vinegar per 2 pt (1 l) of water in the final rinse. This neutralizes the pH, to prevent damage to the fabric. Wash with detergent and hang the fabric out to dry.

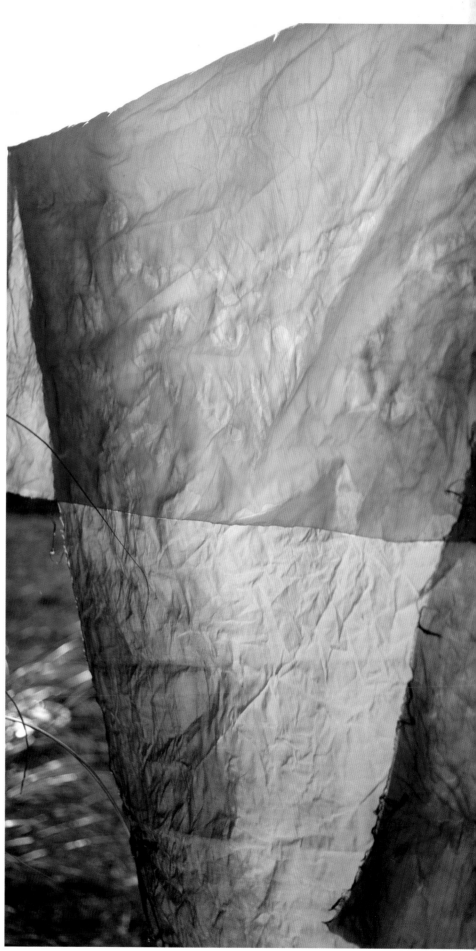

dip-dyed
pashmina shawl

The beauty of indigo and the many shades of blue it can produce can be seen in this project. Any woolen shawl or scarf can be used, with the shading producing a very attractive effect.

You will need
- Pashmina or fine woolen shawl
- Prepared indigo vat (see page 8)
- Rubber gloves and apron
- Bowls for soaking and rinsing
- White household vinegar
- Washing detergent

1 Soak the shawl in clean cold water for a couple of hours.

2 Squeeze out all the excess water and then fold the shawl in half and hold it up so that both fringed ends are hanging down—another pair of hands will make this easier! Wearing rubber gloves, dip the shawl into the indigo vat so that both ends are immersed, with the center section of the shawl above the surface.

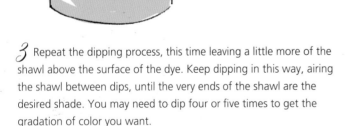

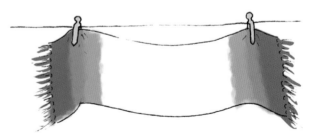

3 Repeat the dipping process, this time leaving a little more of the shawl above the surface of the dye. Keep dipping in this way, airing the shawl between dips, until the very ends of the shawl are the desired shade. You may need to dip four or five times to get the gradation of color you want.

4 Rinse carefully in several changes of cold water until no excess dye remains. Add white vinegar to the final rinse and then wash with detergent. Allow to dry, then press on the correct setting.

dip-dyed
bench pillow

Crisp linen, folded and dipped into the indigo vat and then finished with a freemotion machine-embroidered motif, makes a lovely addition to a garden bench. Here's a simple way to make a zipped pillow with a tidy finish.

You will need
- Prepared indigo vat (see page 8)
- Rubber gloves and apron
- Bowls for soaking and rinsing
- White household vinegar
- Washing detergent
- Two pieces of linen, each measuring 27 x 17 in. (67.5 x 42.5 cm)
- Embellishments such as appliqué or embroidery (optional)
- 27-in. (67.5-cm) zipper
- Pillow form (cushion pad) to fit
- Basic sewing kit
- Sewing machine

1 Soak the linen fabric in clean, cold water for a couple of hours.

2 Remove from the bowl and squeeze out any excess water, then dip-dye the short ends of both pieces of linen, following the instructions on pages 14–15. Make sure you fold the linen in half across its width to dye the two short ends evenly. Rinse, wash, and leave to dry.

3 Once the two dyed pieces are completely dry, press them and add any embellishments to the front, such as appliqué or embroidery, if desired.

4 With right sides together, pin and machine stitch the long side of one of the pieces of linen to one side of the zipper. Repeat with the other piece of linen and the other side of the zipper. Zigzag through both the linen and the edge of the zipper tape to prevent fraying.

5 With the right sides uppermost and the zipper lying horizontally, create a small overlap to conceal the zipper. Pin in place and then machine stitch, using the zipper foot on your sewing machine and following the teeth of the zipper to give a neat finish. Open the zipper.

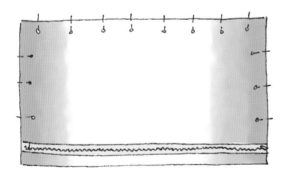

6 Pin the remaining three sides right sides together, with the zipper lying flat to one side. Machine stitch around the edges, taking a ¾-in. (2-cm) seam allowance.

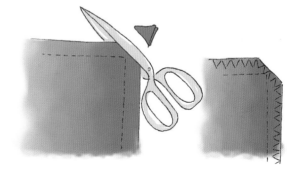

7 Snip the corners to reduce bulk and and zigzag stitch around the seams to neaten. Turn the cover right side out and insert the pillow form (cushion pad).

dip-dyed *lampshade*

Silk is a lovely fabric to work with and indigo works so well with it! Repeated graded dipping can give you a gradual darkening of the shade of blue achieved which produces an attractive finish.

You will need

- Prepared indigo vat (see page 8)
- Rubber gloves and apron
- Bowls for soaking and rinsing
- White household vinegar
- Washing detergent
- Enough plain silk fabric to make one lampshade (refer to your lampshade kit for guidance)
- Drum lampshade kit (see suppliers on page 110)

1 Soak the silk fabric in clean, cold water for a couple of hours.

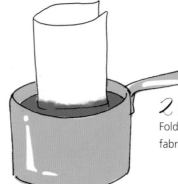

2 Remove from the bowl and squeeze out any excess water. Fold the fabric in half widthways and dip-dye one end of the fabric, following the instructions on pages 14–15.

3 Repeat the dipping process, each time leaving a little more of the fabric out of the vat. This way you will achieve a gradual color change.

4 Rinse carefully in several changes of cold water until no excess dye remains. Add vinegar to the final rinse and then wash with detergent. Allow to dry on the line and then press the fabric carefully.

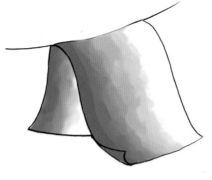

5 Follow the lampshade kit instructions to make up your lampshade. Lampshade kits usually consist of a panel of self-adhesive lampshade PVC, cut to the correct size, two lampshade rings (one with a fitting), and self-adhesive tape.

chapter 2

Shibori Kanoko and Kumo

tie-dyeing with and without stones

Tying bunched fabric in order to prevent the dye from reaching parts of the fabric produces some lovely patterns. This tie-dye effect is very well known, and it works particularly well with indigo. You can also tie stones into the fabric.

shibori kanoko and kumo Techniques

When tie-dyeing, the fabric can just be tied using string or elastic bands at intervals, but a more varied effect can be achieved by wrapping the fabric around stones before soaking and dyeing. The stones can be in a variety of shapes and sizes, for a more random pattern, or similar-sized for a regular pattern. The instructions below are for tie-dyeing with stones, but the technique is just the same if you are tying fabric without stones: simply bunch up your fabric, at regular intervals or in a random pattern, and tie tightly with string or elastic.

You will need
- Fabric
- Selection of stones
- String
- Prepared indigo vat (see page 8)
- Rubber gloves and apron
- Bowls for soaking and rinsing
- White household vinegar
- Washing detergent
- Scissors

1 Gather together your stones, choosing a variety of sizes and shapes depending on the effect you're after. Make sure the stones are clean.

2 Starting in the center of your piece of fabric, wrap the fabric around the first stone and tie very tightly with string.

3 Repeat until you have enough stones tied in place, working outward from the center.

4 Soak the fabric in clean, cold water for a few hours. Remove from the bowl and gently squeeze out all the excess water.

5 Dye the fabric in your prepared indigo vat, following the instructions on pages 12–14. Repeat the dipping process until you have reached the desired shade. Rinse the fabric, adding vinegar to the final rinse, then let it dry.

6 Using scissors, carefully snip the strings holding the stones in place. The undyed fabric will be revealed, forming a ring pattern. These are the areas the dye could not reach. Wash the fabric and dry it.

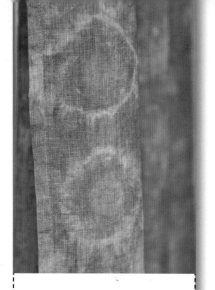

voile *curtain*

Voile curtains with a simple pattern repeated along the hem and leading edge are a charming way to decorate a window. Any bottle top or lid of the same size will create this effect. Using elastic bands makes this a really quick dyeing project to prepare.

You will need

- Bottle tops and elastic bands
- Ready-made voile curtains, pre-washed and dried
- Prepared indigo vat (see page 8)
- Rubber gloves and apron
- Bowls for soaking and rinsing
- White household vinegar
- Washing detergent
- Iron

1 Mark the fabric with pins at regular intervals of about 6 in. (15 cm) along the hem and two places on the leading edges of both voile curtains.

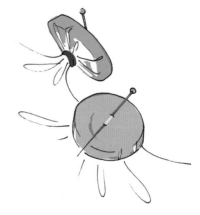

2 At each interval secure the fabric around the bottle tops with elastic bands. Take out the pins

3 Soak, dye, and rinse the fabric, following the instructions on pages 12–14.

4 Once rinsed remove the bands and bottle tops. Wash in detergent before drying thoroughly. Once dry, iron on the correct setting.

striped *linen curtain*

Large pieces of fabric can be tricky to dye in a pan at home, but pleating the fabric and tying it tightly will enable you to dye large, curtain-sized pieces quite easily. Ready-made curtains can also be dyed in this way!

You will need

- Ready-made linen curtain or length of linen, pre-washed and dried (see Calculating fabric, below)
- Elastic or string for the ties
- Prepared indigo vat (see page 8)
- Rubber gloves and apron
- Bowls for soaking and rinsing
- White household vinegar
- Washing detergent

1 Pleat the fabric along its length, keeping the pleats as straight and even as possible.

2 Tie all along this pleated length of fabric, making sure that the ties are tied really tight and are evenly spaced.

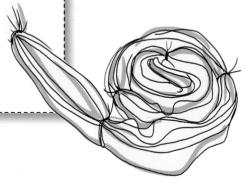

3 Soak the fabric in clean, cold water for a few hours, then squeeze out the excess water. Dye, following the instructions on pages 12–14. Very large pieces of fabric may need to be formed into a coil shape in order to fit into the dyeing vat. Wear rubber gloves and work the fibers under the surface in order to achieve a good color.

Calculating Fabric

Measure the required drop of the curtain and add on 5 in. (12.5 cm) for the hems at the top and bottom. (This is for a standard taped heading.) For the width, each curtain needs to be 1.5–2 times the width of the curtain track before being gathered.

4 Rinse in clean water, adding vinegar to the final rinse. Remove the ties and then wash with detergent in the usual way and allow to dry. Press the fabric and either hang the curtain or follow the instructions in Step 5 to make up.

5 Press 1 in. (2.5 cm) to the wrong side on either side of the fabric, pin, and then machine stitch in place. Press 1 in. (2.5 cm) to the wrong side along the top edge and pin in place. Cut the heading tape to the desired width, adding 1 in. (2.5 cm). Pin along the top of the curtain, folding ½ in. (1 cm) under at each end, and then machine stitch in place. Finally, fold a double 2-in. (5-cm) hem at the bottom of the curtain and either machine or hand stitch in place. Gather the curtain to the desired width and hang.

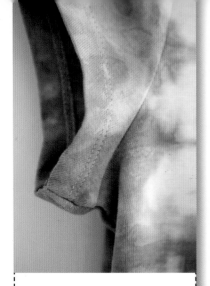

tie-dyed *T-shirt*

An old white or light-colored T-shirt can be given a new lease on life if you tie-dye it! Folding and tying it tightly will give you a random striped effect.

You will need

- Plain, light-colored T-shirt, pre-washed and dried
- Elastic or string for ties
- Prepared indigo vat (see page 8)
- Rubber gloves and apron
- Bowls for soaking and rinsing
- Scissors
- White household vinegar
- Washing detergent

1 Fold the T-shirt into loose pleats. Horizontal folds will produce horizontal stripes.

2 Tie very tightly at intervals across the length of the folded T-shirt. The more ties you use, the paler your T-shirt will be; using fewer ties produces darker results.

3 Soak the tied T-shirt in clean water to prepare it for dyeing. Dye following the instructions on pages 12–14, repeating the dipping until the desired shade is reached.

4 Rinse in plenty of clean water, adding vinegar to the final rinse. Carefully remove the ties with scissors and then wash the T-shirt with washing detergent. Allow to dry.

reversible *Tablecloth*

A tie-dyed tablecloth finished with a patterned bias binding edging—just turn it over for a plain tablecloth!

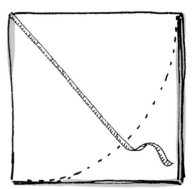

1 Fold your fabric into four and measure along the top of this square of fabric. Use this measurement to draw a curved line from corner to corner from the center of the fabric.

You will need

- Fabric large enough for a tablecloth (see Calculating fabric, below), pre-washed and dried—a large cotton sheet is ideal
- Fabric marker pen
- Basic sewing kit
- Elastic or string for tying
- Prepared indigo vat (see page 8)
- Rubber gloves and apron
- Bowls for soaking and rinsing
- White household vinegar
- Washing detergent
- Patterned bias binding 1 in. (2.5 cm) wide
- Sewing machine
- Iron

2 Keeping the fabric folded, cut through the four layers one at a time, carefully following the marked line. This will give you a perfect circle.

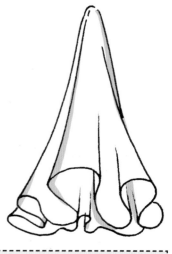

3 Take hold of the center point of the tablecloth and shake the folds out so that the fabric drapes gracefully.

Calculating Fabric

Decide how long you want the drop on your tablecloth to be. This could be anything from 8–12 in. (20–30 cm). Measure the diameter of your table and add twice the desired drop to this measurement—this will be the diameter of your cloth. Cut a square of fabric to this size, adding on ½ in. (1 cm) for seam allowances.

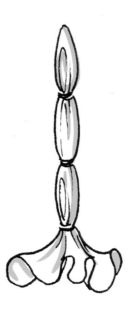

4 Working from the center out toward the edge of the cloth, place ties at irregular intervals along the bundled cloth. This will result in a sunburst pattern. Ensure that the ties are really tight.

5 Soak the tablecloth in clean, cold water for a couple of hours, then squeeze out the excess water. Dye the fabric, following the instructions on pages 12–14. As this is a large piece, you'll need to work the fibers under the surface for a few seconds.

6 Rinse in several changes of clean water, adding vinegar to the final rinse. Remove the ties, wash with detergent, and allow to dry.

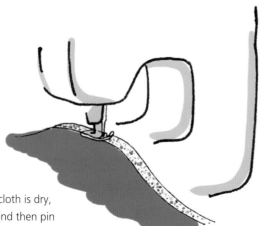

7 When the tablecloth is dry, press with an iron and then pin one raw edge of the bias binding around the edge of the entire cloth. Machine stitch in place, stitching ¼ in. (6 mm) from the edge and removing the pins as you go.

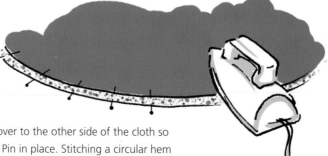

8 Press the entire bias binding over to the other side of the cloth so that it is only visible on one side. Pin in place. Stitching a circular hem can be tricky and using this technique helps to get a good, neat finish! Topstitch the binding to the other side and remove the pins.

Table runner

A table runner is a quick and simple way to dress a table stylishly.
Using stones tied tightly into linen produces some gorgeous patterns.

1 Select stones in a variety of sizes and shapes in order to give you an interesting and varied effect.

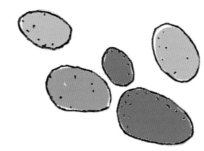

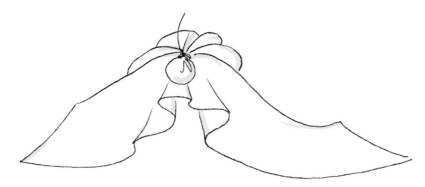

2 Take your piece of linen and, starting in the center, bunch the linen around one of the stones and tie very tightly with string.

You will need

- Undyed linen fabric, approx. 15 in. (38 cm) wide by the length of your table plus 4 in. (10 cm)
- Selection of stones
- String for tying
- Prepared indigo vat (see page 8)
- Bowls for soaking and rinsing
- Rubber gloves and apron
- White household vinegar
- Washing detergent
- Iron
- Basic sewing kit

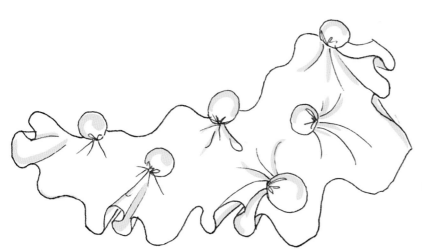

3 Repeat with more stones, spacing them as evenly as you can until you have enough stones tied in place.

4 Soak the linen in clean, cold water for a few hours.

5 Remove the linen from the water, squeeze gently to remove some of the excess water, and dye following the instructions on pages 12–14. Repeat the dipping process until you have reached the desired shade.

6 Rinse in several changes of clean water, adding vinegar to the final rinse. Using scissors, snip the strings holding the stones in place. The undyed fabric around the stones will be revealed in a pretty ring pattern. Wash in detergent and allow to dry, then iron on the correct setting.

7 Once dried and pressed, trim away any frayed edges using scissors and cut to size.

8 Press and turn over a double 1-in. (2.5-cm) hem on all four sides before machine stitching in place.

wall *hanging*

Tying the fabric from the center outward produces a dramatic "sunburst" pattern. Hang the dyed and stitched fabric on a rod to make it into an attractive wall hanging.

1 Decide what size you want your wall hanging to be and cut the fabric to this size, remembering to add 2 in. (5 cm) to the width and 2–3 in. (5–7.5 cm) to the length for the hems and rod casing. (The depth of the casing will depend on the size of the hanging rod.) Find the approximate center of the fabric by holding it in one hand and shaking it, allowing it to drape and fall into irregular pleats.

2 Starting at the center, tie tight ties along the length of the bunched fabric.

3 Soak in clean water for a few hours and then dip into the prepared indigo vat until the desired shade is achieved.

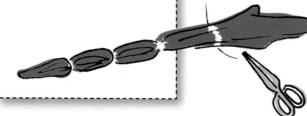

4 Rinse in plenty of clean, cold water until all the excess dye is removed, adding vinegar to the final rinse. Remove the ties, wash the dyed fabric with washing detergent, and allow to dry.

5 Leaving the top edge for now, press and then machine stitch a double ½-in. (1-cm) hem along the sides and bottom.

6 Making sure that it is large enough to allow your pole or rod to be inserted, machine stitch a deeper double hem along the top edge of the fabric. Insert the pole or rod and then hang.

chapter 3

Shibori Itajime

tie-dyeing with wood

This technique uses pieces of wood or heavy cardstock (card) to clamp pleated fabric tightly before dyeing in order to prevent the dye from reaching all of the fabric. Because the fabric is folded many times to fit the size of the clamp, this is a great way to dye quite large pieces of fabric easily.

shibori itajime Techniques

This technique produces a light and open pattern with attractive repeats—particularly if the fabric is pleated vertically along its length. You can also vary the effect by pleating again across these pleats horizontally or diagonally. The pleated fabric is then placed between two pieces of wood and the whole thing is tied together tightly with string. As the items are only dipped into the indigo dye vat for a few moments, heavy card stock can also be used to hold the fabric in place. After dipping and airing, the items must remain clamped until after the final rinse in order to prevent any dye from seeping into the undyed parts within the clamps.

You will need

- Two pieces of wood or heavy cardstock (card)
- String
- Prepared indigo vat (see page 8)
- Rubber gloves and apron
- Bowls for soaking and rinsing
- White household vinegar
- Washing detergent

1 Fold the fabric into vertical pleats, then pleat again across the width. This will produce a checked pattern. The folded piece should be slightly wider than your pieces of wood or cardstock (card)—the amount of fabric exposed at the sides, top, and bottom will dictate how broad or narrow your stripes will be.

2 Place the pleated fabric between the two pieces of wood.

3 Tie string tightly around the wood-and-fabric sandwich.

4 Soak in cold, clean water for a few hours. The wood will float, so weigh it down with something like a brick.

5 Squeeze as much water out of the fabric as possible. Dip into the indigo vat by sliding the prepared fabric down the side of the pan; remember, you are aiming to disturb the surface as little as possible (see pages 12–14). Remove after a few moments, letting the excess dye dribble back into the vat with as little splashing as possible.

6 Allow the dyed fabric to air—still clamped between the wood—opening the edges of the pleats to allow oxygen to develop the dye. Repeat the dipping process if you want a deeper shade of blue, airing and allowing the dye to develop each time.

7 With the fabric still clamped and tied, rinse well in several changes of cold, clean water, adding vinegar to the final rinse (see pages 12–14).

8 Cut the tied string and remove the wood.

9 Unfold the pleated fabric, wash in detergent and allow to dry.

room *divider*

Large-scale pieces of fabric such as these room dividers provide the perfect opportunity to show off this pattern, created by "clamping" folded fabric between wooden laundry pegs.

You will need

- Two pieces of fabric, each measuring 44 x 24 in. (110 x 60 cm)
- Two pieces of fabric, each measuring 44 x 52 in. (110 x 130 cm)
- Wooden pegs
- Prepared indigo vat (see page 8)
- Rubber gloves and apron
- Bowls for soaking and rinsing
- White household vinegar
- Washing detergent
- Sewing machine
- Basic sewing kit
- Wooden rod to fit across your room

1 Take the smaller pieces of fabric and fold each one in half—short sides together—and then in half again (the larger pieces need no preparation). Place the pegs along the longer folded sides as shown, three along one side and four along the other.

2 Dye and rinse the fabric, including the larger pieces, following the instructions on pages 12–14. Only remove the pegs once the fabric is well rinsed. When dry, iron the fabric on the correct setting.

3 Join the longer edge of each of the small pieces of fabric to the short edges of the large pieces using a flat fell seam: first place the two pieces wrong sides together and machine stitch, taking a 1½-in. (4-cm) seam allowance. Trim one seam allowance to ½ in. (1 cm). Open out the fabric and press the seam so the wider seam allowance lies on top of the trimmed one. Tuck the wider seam allowance under by ½ in. (1 cm) press, then machine stitch close to the pressed fold.

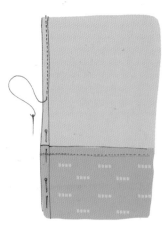

4 Hem the side seams by turning over a double 1-in. (2.5-cm) hem to the wrong side and machine stitching in place.

5 Repeat to create a hem along the bottom. Then turn over a double 1½ in. (4 cm) hem to the wrong side and stitch to create a channel for the wooden rod across the top of each divider.

garden *canopy*

A freestanding awning for the garden, propped up on bamboo canes, makes the perfect place to rest, recline, and read while shaded from the sun!

You will need

- 1¾ x 4¼ yds (1.5 x 3.8 m) linen fabric
- Two pieces of wood, approx. 8½ x 11 x ¾ in. (22 x 28 x 2 cm)
- String
- Prepared indigo vat (see page 8)
- Rubber gloves and apron
- Bowls for soaking and rinsing
- White household vinegar
- Washing detergent
- 20 in. (50 cm) webbing tape cut into four equal pieces
- Basic sewing kit
- Reel of seam binding tape
- Four garden canes, cut down to preferred height
- Mallet
- Eight tent pegs
- 22 yds (20 m) thin rope or piping cord

1 Fold the fabric vertically into pleats a little wider than the wood, then fold the bottom right corner over to the left-hand edge to form a triangle. Keep folding the fabric over in triangles until you reach the end. This will create the diagonal lines. Clamp between the pieces of wood, then soak and dye, along with the webbing tape, following the instructions on pages 45–47. Rinse, wash, allow to dry, then press.

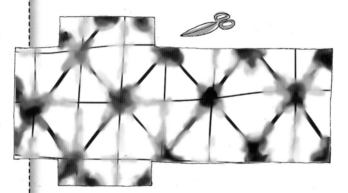

2 Cut the dyed fabric as shown. The long bottom part of the cross will be the height of your canopy.

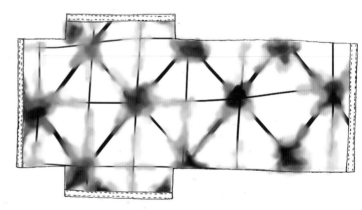

3 Hem the four sides using seam binding tape (see page 105).

4 Fold each piece of dyed webbing tape in half and insert into the corner seams, as shown. The raw edges should be lined up and the folded edge facing away from the seam. Pin in place.

5 With right sides together, stitch down each of the four corner seams, taking a ¾-in. (2-cm) seam allowance.

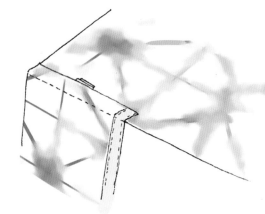

6 Press the stitched seams over to one side, in each case folding away from the short side.

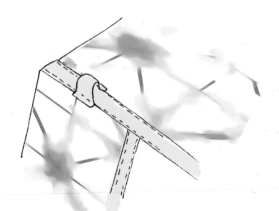

7 Cut four strips of seam binding, each 2½ in. (6 cm) long. Cover the raw edges of the canop with seam binding and stitch in place. Then position the 2½-in. (6-cm) strips of seam binding over the seam binding near the top of the canopy to form "loops," tucking the raw edges in on each side. These loops will hold the garden canes in position once the canopy is erected.

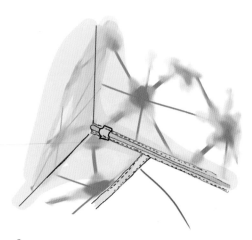

8 Turn the canopy right side out and place the four canes in the loops of seam binding, one at each corner.

9 Using a mallet, bash the tent pegs firmly into the ground. Tie the ropes through the webbing loops and then loosely onto the pegs. Pull the ropes firmly and adjust pegs, canes, and ropes as needed before knotting the ropes tightly.

linen *skirt*

This simple wraparound skirt is both easy to make and easy to wear, and the perfect choice for hot summer days! The pattern produced by folding and clamping the fabric is regular and pleasing.

You will need

- Length of undyed fabric (see Calculating fabric, below)
- Two pieces of wood, approximately 4 x 6 x ¾ in. (10 x 15 x 2 cm)
- String
- Prepared indigo vat (see page 8)
- Rubber gloves and apron
- Bowls for soaking and rinsing
- White household vinegar
- Washing detergent
- Basic sewing kit
- Sewing machine

1 Fold the fabric vertically into pleats a little wider than the wood, then pleat it horizontally. Clamp, soak, and dye the fabric, following the instructions on pages 45–47. Rinse, wash, allow to dry, and press. Trim away any frayed edges.

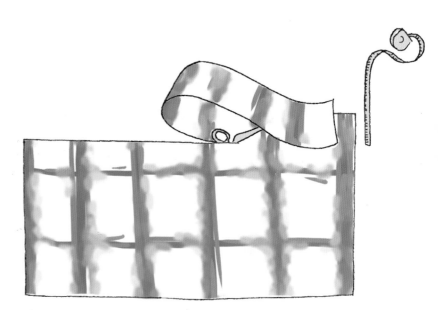

2 Measure and cut a strip of fabric 6 in. (15 cm) deep from one of the long edges.

Calculating Fabric

Decide how long you want the skirt to be and measure from your waist to this point. Add on 3 in. (8 cm) for the top and bottom hems and another 6 in. (15 cm) for the waist ties.

Measure one and a half times around your waist and add on 3 in. (8 cm) for the side hems.

Cut the fabric to these measurements.

3 Fold this strip of fabric in half lengthwise and then fold both raw edges under and stitch close to the fold. Cut this in half to create two ties.

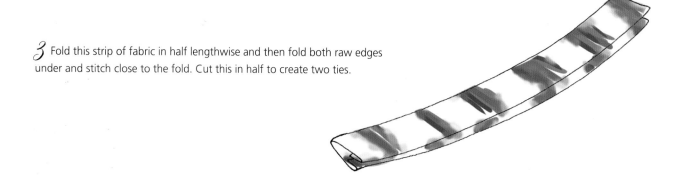

4 Turn a double ¾-in. (2-cm) hem along both side edges and along the bottom hem of the skirt. Using the zigzag setting on your sewing machine, stitch along the top of the skirt.

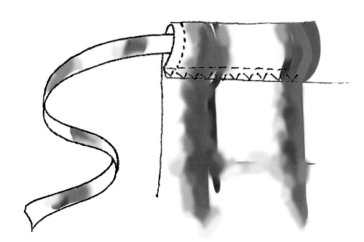

5 Turn the zigzag edge over to the wrong side of the skirt, creating a hem of 2 in. (5 cm) and insert the end of one tie into each end of the waist channel, as shown. Straight stitch with the sewing machine down each short side of the channel, trapping the ties in place, and along the long edge, just above the zigzag stitching.

6 To wear, wrap the skirt around the waist and tie at the side.

silk *scarf*

Silk scarf blanks are available from craft and dye shops. Clamping the silk between pieces of wood after pleating produces a subtle effect with a regular pattern.

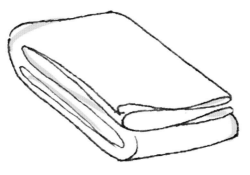

1 Fold the scarf vertically into pleats a little wider than the wood and then pleat horizontally.

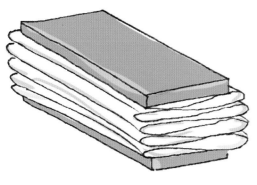

2 Place the pleated scarf between the two pieces of wood.

You will need

- Silk scarf, pre-washed and dried
- Two pieces of wood, approximately 6 x 3 x ¾ in. (15 x 8 x 2 cm)
- String
- Scissors
- Prepared indigo vat (see page 8)
- Rubber gloves and apron
- Bowls for soaking and rinsing
- White household vinegar
- Washing detergent

3 Tie the two pieces of wood together with string. Tie tightly and knot the ends securely so that the scarf is clamped inside. Soak in a bowl or bucket of clean, cold water—you may need to weigh the wood down with a brick as the wood will float!

4 Remove from the water and squeeze to remove some of the excess water. Place in your prepared indigo vat to dye the fabric. Dip several times, allowing the dye to develop each time, until the desired shade is achieved.

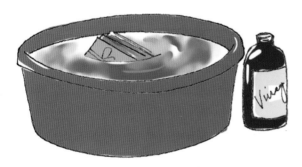

5 Rinse several times in clean, cold water, remembering to add vinegar to the final rinse.

6 Cut the string and remove the two pieces of wood to reveal the areas of undyed fabric. Shake out the scarf, wash in detergent, and hang on the line to dry.

swedish
roll-up shade

A simple roll-up covering looks great at any window. The regular open pattern produced when dyeing fabric pleated and clamped between wood works well with this style of shade.

1 Fold the fabric vertically into pleats a little wider than the wood, then pleat it horizontally. Clamp, soak, and dye the fabric, following the instructions on pages 45–47. Allow to dry, press, and trim away any frayed edges.

You will need

- Length of undyed fabric (see Calculating fabric, below)
- Two pieces of wood approximately 6 x 3 x ¾ in. (15 x 8 x 2 cm)
- String
- Prepared indigo vat (see page 8)
- Rubber gloves and apron
- Bowls for soaking and rinsing
- White household vinegar
- Washing detergent
- Basic sewing kit
- Sewing machine
- Two D-rings
- Hook-and-loop tape, 1 in. (2.5 cm) shorter than the width of your blind
- Wooden lathe, 1 in.(2.5 cm) shorter than the width of your shade
- 1 x 1 in. (2.5 x 2.5 cm) wooden batten, 1 in.(2.5 cm) shorter than the width of your blind
- Staple gun
- 2 brass screw eyes
- Thin cord or twine
- Cleat for the cord

2 Turn a double 1-in. (2.5-cm) hem to the wrong side on both sides of the fabric and stitch these side seams in place. Turn a double 2-in. (5-cm) to the wrong side along the bottom edge and stitch close to the fold to create a channel for the wooden lathe.

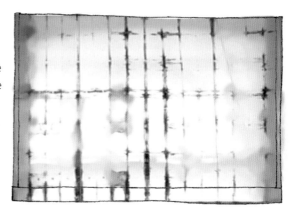

3 Cut a 6-in. (15-cm) strip off the top of your dyed fabric and use it to cut two rectangles, each 6 x 4 in. (15 x 10 cm). Fold each rectangle in half lengthwise and then turn both raw edges under and machine stitch along the open long edge to create two tabs.

Calculating Fabric

Decide how long and wide you want the finished shade to be; it's up to you whether you hang the shade on the inside or the outside of the window recess. Add 4 in. (10 cm) to the width to allow for the side hems and 10 in. (25 cm) to the length to allow for the top and bottom hems, plus the fabric needed for the tabs (see step 3, overleaf).

4 Place each tab through a D-ring and pin so the raw edges line up with each other.

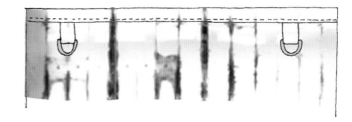

5 Pin the D-ring tabs in place along the top of the fabric, right sides together and with raw edges level and approximately 10 in. (25 cm) in from each outside edge. Take the loop side of the hook-and-loop tape and pin it along the top of the shade, over the D-ring tabs. Stitch the lower edge (nearest to the tabs) only.

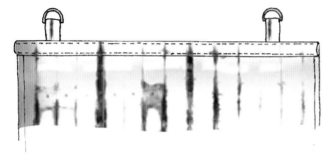

6 Fold the hook-and-loop tape over to the wrong side of the shade and stitch along the bottom edge of the tape, ensuring that the D-ring tabs are clear of the stitch line.

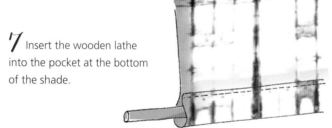

7 Insert the wooden lathe into the pocket at the bottom of the shade.

8 Attach the hook side of the hook-and-loop tape to the wooden batten with a staple gun. Fix the screw eyes into the underside of the wooden batten, so that they are in line with the D-ring tabs on the shade. Tie the cord ends to these screw eyes and bring them down behind the shade and up the front, threading them through the D-rings and down to the side where the cleat is positioned.

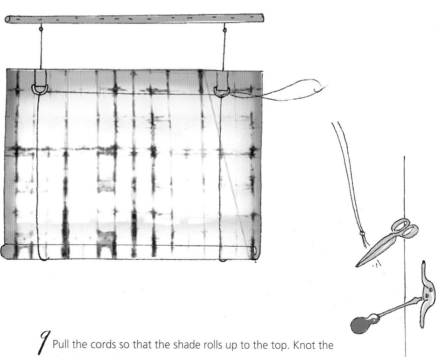

9 Pull the cords so that the shade rolls up to the top. Knot the cord ends together, trimming away any excess cord a little below the knot. Fix the cleat to the wall or window frame as desired.

quilted *placemats*

Quilting is easier than most people think, and pinning and stitching with care will give a neat finish. A contrast patterned binding sets off the blue and white dyed fabric perfectly!

You will need

- 28 x 10 in. (70 x 25 cm) white cotton fabric per mat
- Two pieces of wood approximately 10 x 3 x ¾ in. (25 x 7.5 x 2 cm)
- String
- Prepared indigo vat (see page 8)
- Rubber gloves and apron
- Bowls for soaking and rinsing
- White household vinegar
- Washing detergent
- Basic sewing kit
- Sewing machine
- 14 x 10 in. (35 x 25 cm) batting (wadding) per mat
- Small plate or saucer
- Pencil
- 1¾ yds (1½ m) floral bias binding, 1 in. (2.5 cm) wide

1 Fold the fabric vertically into pleats a little wider than the wood, then pleat it horizontally. Clamp, soak, and dye the fabric, following the instructions on pages 45–47. Rinse, adding vinegar to the final rinse. Wash in detergent, dry, and press.

2 Cut the fabric in half to give two 14 x 10-in. (35 x 25-cm) rectangles. Place one piece on your work surface, with the batting (wadding) on top, then place the remaining piece on top of the batting. Pin all three layers together.

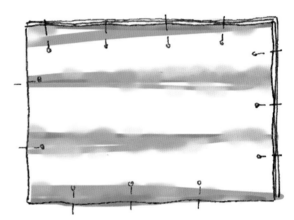

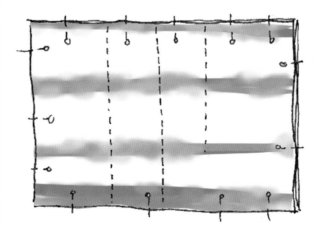

3 Using a straight stitch on your sewing machine, quilt vertical lines through all three layers, starting from the center and working outward.

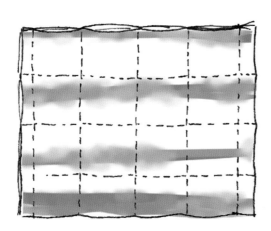

4 Repeat to quilt the horizontal lines across the mat, again starting from center and working out toward the outside edges. This will prevent the layers from moving about too muc and also adds visual interesth.

5 Use a small plate or saucer to draw a curved edge at each of the four corners. Trim away the excess fabric, including any layers that may have moved during quilting.

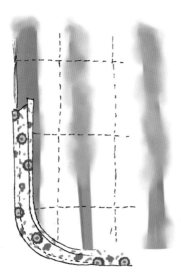

6 Stitch one edge of the bias binding all around the upper edge of the front of the placemat, starting and finishing at the center of one of the long sides. Finish by neatly folding one end of the bias binding under and tucking the other end inside before stitching over the join.

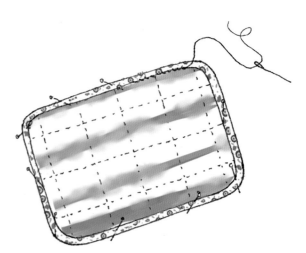

7 Fold the bias binding over to the back of the mat, pin, and neatly stitch it in place.

chapter 4

Shibori Arashi

tie-dyeing with tubes

A dramatic effect can be achieved on narrower pieces of fabric by using a piece of plastic tubing. Fabric is wrapped loosely around the tube and tied in place with string; the fabric is then pushed down to one end. The dye can only get to the areas of fabric on the outside of the folds, which creates a crisp, attractive pattern.

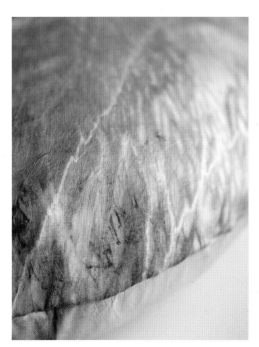

shibori arashi Techniques

Depending on how many times you wrap the fabric around the tube, and how tight the folds are, you can create a variety of patterns using this method. The fabric nearest the tube will have the faintest pattern, while that on the outside will be a darker blue. The fabric within the folds will remain undyed.

You will need

- Fabric
- 18 in. (45 cm) plastic tube, 3in. (8 cm) in diameter
- String
- Prepared indigo vat (see page 8)
- Rubber gloves and apron
- Bowls for soaking and rinsing
- White household vinegar
- Washing detergent

1 Wrap your fabric widthways around the tube and loosely tie with string in a criss-cross pattern up and down the tube.

2 Push the fabric and string all the way down to one end of the tube, as far as it will go.

3 Soak in cold, clean water for a couple of hours, and squeeze out any excess water.

4 Dye in your prepared indigo vat, following the instructions for plain dyeing on pages 12–14.

5 Rinse several times in clean, cold water, adding vinegar to the final rinse. Carefully cut through the string, unwrap the fabric, wash in detergent, and allow to dry.

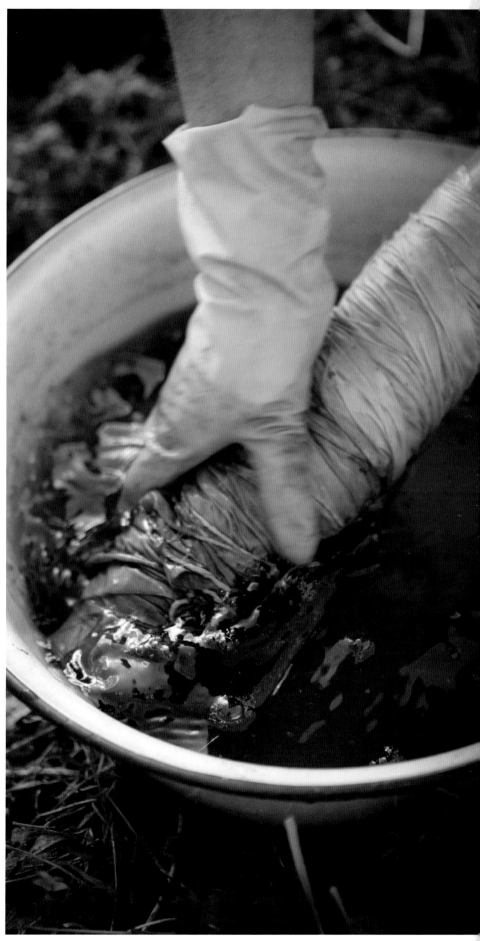

bolster *pillow*

Bolster cushions are always a welcoming addition to a sofa or armchair, tucking in just where you need them. This one is simple to make using a slipstitch to close, with no need of a zipped opening.

1 Prepare and dye the fabric, following the instructions on page 70–71. When dry, iron the fabric on the correct setting.

You will need

- 18 in. (45 cm) plastic tube, 2½ in. (6 cm) in diameter
- String
- 1 yd (90 cm) fabric, 36 in. (90 cm) wide, pre-washed and dried
- Prepared indigo vat (see page 8)
- Rubber gloves and apron
- Bowls for soaking and rinsing
- White household vinegar
- Washing detergent
- Iron
- 1½ yds (1.3 m) piping cord, cut into two
- Sewing machine
- Basic sewing kit
- Bolster pillow form (cushion pad), approximately 6 x 18 in. (15 x 45 cm)

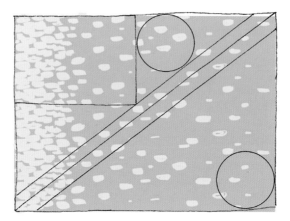

2 Lay your fabric out flat. Using the diagram as a guide, cut out the following pieces: one rectangle measuring 20 x 18 in. (50 x 45 cm), two circles measuring 6 in. (15 cm) in diameter, and two strips of fabric on the bias, each approximately 1¼ in. (4 cm) wide.

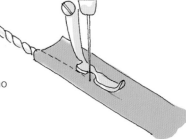

3 Using the piping or zipper foot on your sewing machine, use the strips of bias-cut fabric to cover both pieces of piping cord (see page 106). There should be no need to join strips.

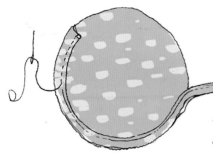

4 Stitch the prepared piping onto the circles, using a sewing machine with a piping foot (or backstitch by hand—see page 107). Start and finish at the center bottom of each circle, folding and overlapping the fabric for a neat join (see page 106).

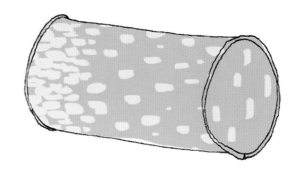

5 With right sides together, pin and stitch the longest sides of the rectangular piece to the piped circles, again starting and finishing at the center bottom. Leave a few inches either side of the join unstitched; this will be stitched later.

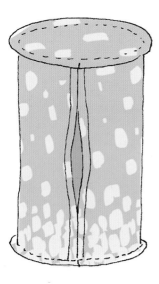

6 Change the foot on your sewing machine to a presser foot and stitch together the long vertical seam that sits at the bottom of the bolster using a straight stitch. Leave a gap of around 6 in. (15 cm) through which you can insert the pillow form (cushion pad) later. Gently press the seam open. Stitch closed the circular ends, trimming away any waste fabric.

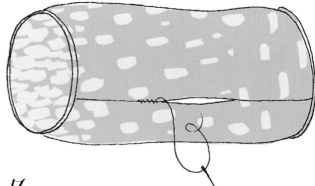

7 Turn the cover right side out before inserting the pillow form. Pin and slipstitch the opening closed (see page 107).

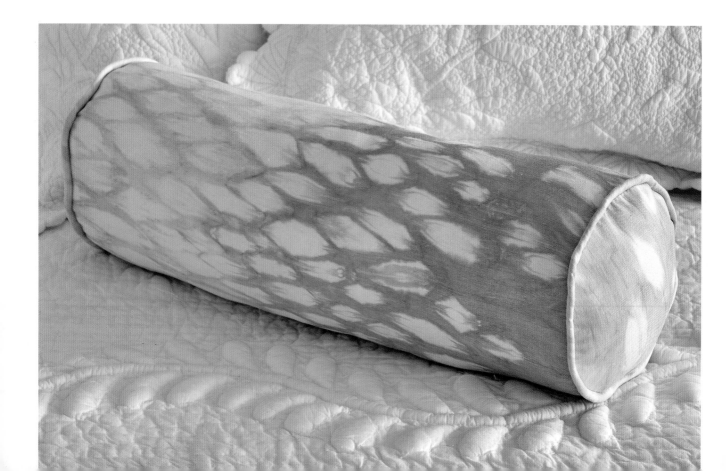

closet *liner*

Usually fabric used behind the glass in closet doors is gathered up, but here the fabric is used flat to show off the beautiful patterns achieved using this simple technique. A fresh indigo vat will give a dark indigo blue to show a crisp pattern!

1 Dye the fabric, following the instructions on pages 70–71. When dry, iron on the correct setting.

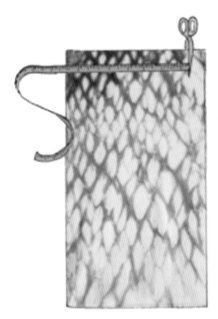

2 Measure the windows of your closet or cupboard and add 4 in. (10 cm) to both the width and the drop. This is to allow for the wire or rod pockets and side hems. Cut two pieces of dyed fabric to these measurements.

You will need

- Fine cotton fabric
- 18 in. (45 cm) plastic tube, 3in. (8 cm) in diameter
- String
- Prepared indigo vat (see page 8)
- Rubber gloves and apron
- Bowls for soaking and rinsing
- White household vinegar
- Washing detergent
- Basic sewing kit
- Four pieces of net wire, cut to just wider than your closet liners
- Eight screw eyes

3 Turn a double 1-in. (2.5-cm) hem to the wrong side on both sides of the fabric, press, and machine stitch in place.

4 Turn a double 1-in. (2.5-cm) hem to the wrong side at both the top and bottom of the fabric to form two channels. Pin and then stitch in place, close to the fold. Thread the net wires or rods through the channels at the top and bottom.

5 Fix screw eyes to the inside of the doors to attach the closet liners to, which should lie flat as opposed to gathered to allow you to see the beautiful patterns produced by this dyeing technique.

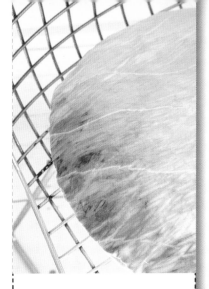

round pillow *cover*

Silk takes indigo dye on beautifully and, as it's quite a fine fabric, it also works well with this "arashi" style of tie-dyeing. The more the fabric is scrunched down the tubes it's wrapped around, the better!

You will need

- Two pieces of silk, each measuring at least 25 x 25 in. (62.5 x 62.5 cm)
- 18 in. (45 cm) plastic tube, 3 in. (8 cm) in diameter
- String
- Prepared indigo vat (see page 8)
- Rubber gloves and apron
- Bowls for soaking and rinsing
- White household vinegar
- Washing detergent
- Large sheet of newspaper
- Pencil and ruler
- Scissors
- Sewing machine
- Basic sewing kit
- 18-in. (45-cm) pillow form (cushion pad)

1 Tie and dye the silk fabric, following the instructions on pages 70–71. When dry, carefully iron the silk on the correct setting.

2 Fold the newspaper into four. Using a ruler, mark the paper at several intervals 9 in. (23 cm) from the center. Cut along these marked points and open the newspaper out to create a large circle.

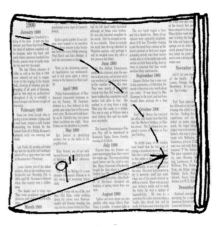

3 Pin the pattern onto one of the pieces of silk and cut out.

4 Fold the second piece of silk in half. Fold the paper pattern in half and place it on the folded silk, 4 in. (10 cm) away from the folded edge of the fabric. Pin in place

5 Starting from the folded edge of the fabric, cut out the elongated semicircle shape.

6 Now cut along the folded edge to create two elongated semicircles and sew a double 1-in. (2.5-cm) hem along both straight edges.

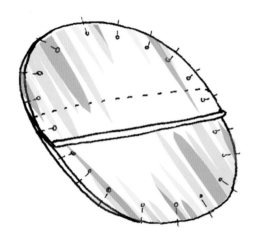

7 Place the hemmed pieces on top of the circle of fabric, right sides together, and with the hemmed edges overlapping. Pin in place.

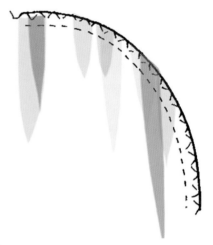

8 Machine stitch around the circle, taking a ¾-in. (2-cm) seam allowance. Trim any excess fabric and finish the seams with a zigzag stitch. Turn the cover right side out and insert the pillow form (cushion pad).

drawstring *bag*

Heavy calico is used here and the paler parts of the bag are produced when the fabric is rolled around the tube. The undyed parts are closest to the tube, with the heavily patterned parts being produced on the outside as the fabric is scrunched up at one end before dipping.

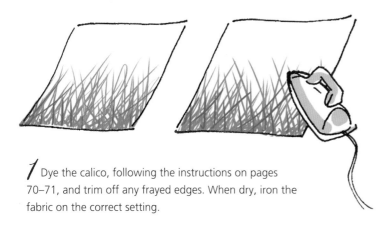

1 Dye the calico, following the instructions on pages 70–71, and trim off any frayed edges. When dry, iron the fabric on the correct setting.

You will need

- Two pieces of calico, each measuring 20 x 20 in. (50 x 50 cm)
- 18 in. (45 cm) plastic tube, 3 in. (8 cm) in diameter
- String
- Prepared indigo vat (see page 8)
- Rubber gloves and apron
- Bowls for soaking and rinsing
- White household vinegar
- Washing detergent
- Sewing machine
- Basic sewing kit
- Piping cord for the drawstring

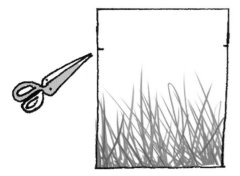

2 Measure 4 in. (10 cm) down from the top of each fabric piece and make a horizontal cut, 1 in. (2.5 cm) long at this marked point on either side of the fabric.

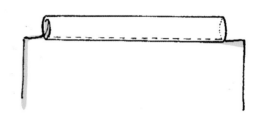

3 On the wrong side of the fabric, fold the fabric above the cuts in toward the center of the fabric piece and press with an iron. Repeat with the other piece of fabric.

4 Fold the top over to the wrong side by 2 in. (5 cm), press, then fold over again to make a double 2-in. (5-cm) hem. Machine stitch in place. This will be the channel for the drawstring. Repeat on the other piece of fabric.

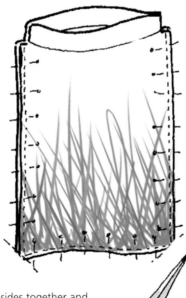

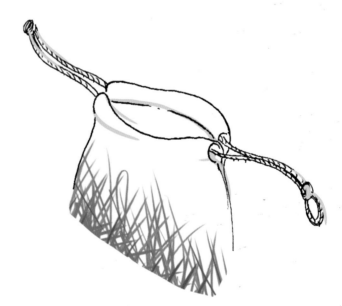

5 Pin the two sides right sides together and machine stitch the two sides and the bottom of the bag. Finish with a zigzag stitch and trim the two bottom corners (see page 106).

6 Turn the bag right side out. Cut two long pieces of piping cord, and thread one through each channel before knotting them together at the ends.

zipped *silk bag*

This is an endlessly useful and easily adapted pattern! Zipped bags of all sizes are quickly made and perfect for pens, cosmetics, knitting supplies, and books.

1 Dye the silk, following the instructions on pages 70–71.

You will need

- Silk fabric, measuring approximately 13 x 18 in. (33 x 45 cm)
- 18 in. (45 cm) plastic tube, 3in. (8 cm) in diameter
- String
- Prepared indigo vat (see page 8)
- Rubber gloves and apron
- Bowls for soaking and rinsing
- White household vinegar
- Washing detergent
- Basic sewing kit
- 10-in. (25-cm) zipper
- Sewing machine with a zipper/ piping foot

2 Once the silk has dried, gently press (make sure the iron is at the correct setting for your fabric) and cut the fabric to 12 x 17 in. (30 x 42.5cm). This will give you a bag measuring 10 x 8 in. (25 x 20 cm).

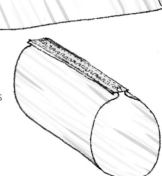

3 Open the zipper and pin one side of the zipper to one of the short ends of the fabric, right sides together, with the underside of the zipper facing upward. Using the zipper foot on your sewing machine, stitch in place. Repeat to attach the other side of the zipper to the other short edge. You should now have a "tube" of fabric, joined together by the zipper. Change to a flat seam foot and zigzag stitch these two edges to prevent fraying.

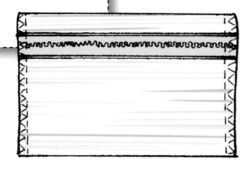

4 With the bag still inside out, position the fabric so that the zipper is approximately 1½ in. (4 cm) down from the top and pin along the sides. Machine stitch down both sides, taking a ½-in. (1-cm) seam allowance, and then zigzag stitch the raw edges.

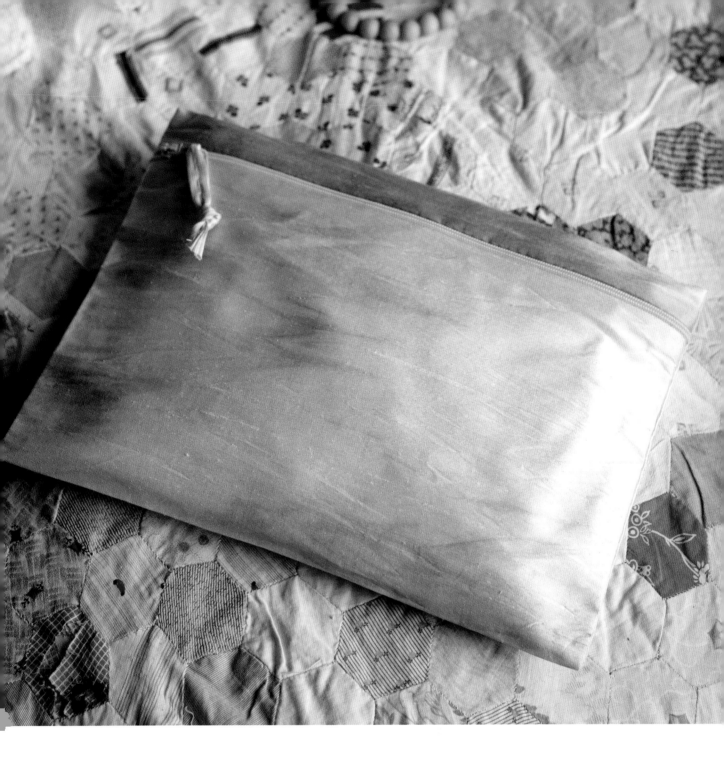

5 Turn the bag right side out through the opened zipper. Make a zipper pull: take a strip of fabric and fold both raw edges in toward the center. Fold in half lengthways to conceal the raw edges and topstitch to secure. Knot through the zipper head as shown.

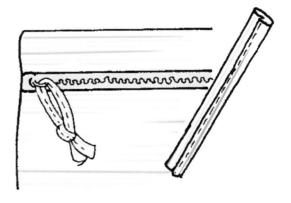

chapter 5

Shibori Nui

sewn and gathered fabric dyeing

Shibori nui, or stitched shibori, is a technique that uses stitching to gather up the fabric, creating areas that are resistant to the indigo dye. The resistant areas will keep the original color while all the exposed areas will become a beautiful indigo blue!

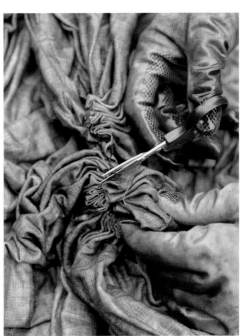

shibori nui Techniques

Preparing fabric for dyeing by stitching and gathering areas of fabric can be a little time-consuming but the intricate patterns achieved make it time well spent! Some great patterns can be created using a plain running stitch. Vary this by folding or pleating before stitching and then gathering up tightly. Pinching the fabric along pattern lines and stitching a ridge of fabric before gathering up gives a lovely effect and shows off the shades of indigo perfectly! Use a strong thread, something that will cope with being pulled hard as it gathers the fabric into tight bundles. Work with short lengths of stitching to help prevent the thread from wearing and snapping during the dyeing process.

Straight stitching

Straight stitched patterns using an outline of an image can produce some lovely results like the flower pattern on the apron on page 98.

You will need
- Fabric
- Strong thread
- Hand sewing needle
- Pencil
- Ruler
- Scissors
- Prepared indigo vat (see page 8)
- Rubber gloves and apron
- Bowls for soaking and rinsing
- White household vinegar
- Washing detergent

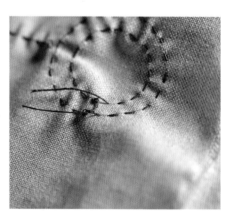

1 Trace an image onto the fabric using an ordinary pencil. Start stitching along these lines in an even running stitch, making sure there is a firm knot at the beginning of the stitching. Leave the end of the thread trailing free. If your pattern has parallel lines of stitching, make sure you start and end at the same position.

2 Once all the stitching is complete, pull all the free ends to gather up the fabric. Tie the free ends together firmly so the fabric stays gathered up tight during dyeing. It is now ready to be soaked in cold water in preparation for dyeing.

Pinching and stitching

Pinching the fabric and then stitching along the ridge of fabric leaves a lovely crisp design.

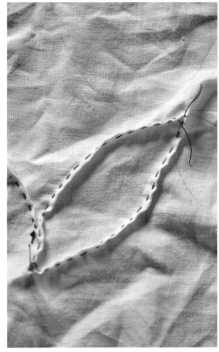

1 Transfer the design onto your fabric with an ordinary pencil. Pinch the fabric along the lines as you sew a row of small even running stitches. Make sure that each line of stitching starts with a firm knot and finishes with a free end for pulling up later.

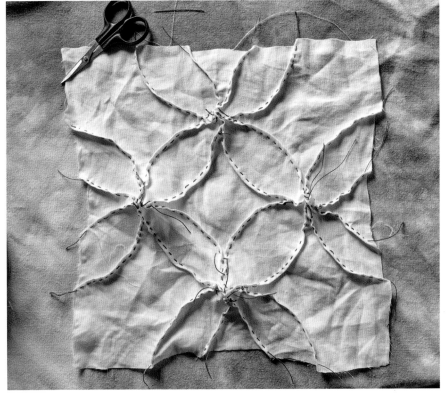

2 Complete all the stitching before pulling up and gathering the fabric. It is important that the lines of stitching do not cross over each other, so at times these rows of stitching can be quite short.

3 Gather the fabric along the stitch lines by pulling on the free ends of thread, then tie off tightly. Once all the ends are tied off tightly the fabric is ready to be soaked in cold water in preparation for dyeing.

Folding and stitching
Folding and stitching rows of fabric evenly produces neat little stripes!

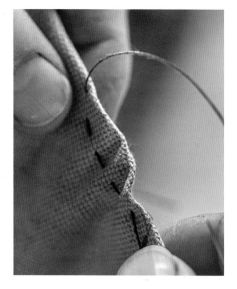

1 Fold the fabric. Start with a firm knot as before and, using a small even running stitch, sew along the fold, keeping the stitches close to the folded edge.

2 Stitch the rows below leaving a gap of ¼ in. (5 mm) between each one. Each stitch should be directly in line with the one above in order to create neat stripes. Leave the free ends of thread trailing when you finish.

3 Complete all the stitching before pulling up the threads to gather the fabric up tightly. Tie the free ends tightly together so that the fabric is held firmly pleated during dyeing. The fabric is now ready to be soaked in cold water in preparation for dyeing.

Dyeing and finishing stitched fabric

Stitched and gathered fabric is soaked and dyed in the usual way—it is important to keep all the stitches in until the dye is rinsed out to keep the dye away from the undyed parts.

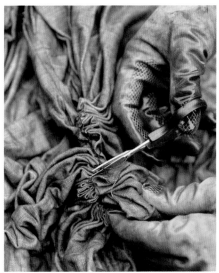

1 Soak the stitched fabric in cold water for a few hours, then squeeze out as much water as you can as too much water can shorten the length of time the dye vat will be effective.

2 Dye the fabric in your prepared indigo vat, following the instructions on pages 12–14. Repeat the dipping process until you have reached the desired shade. Rinse the fabric, adding vinegar to the final rinse, then carefully snip the threads.

3 Pull apart the gathers and remove threads, then wash and dry the fabric.

easy *roman shade*

This is a really simple way to make a shade that has no need for rods, and allows the light to shine through the patterns created by stitching and gathering fabric before dyeing. It is a simple and quick way to produce something for your home that is both beautiful and unique!

1 Fold the fabric over lengthwise so that the two sides meet each other at the center. Using long running stitches about ½ in. (1 cm) long, evenly stitch about ½ in. (1 cm) from each folded edge, so you stitch through two layers of fabric. Pull up the stitched fabric into tight gathers and secure the ends. Soak, dye, and rinse the fabric, following the instructions on page 91. Once dry, press the fabric.

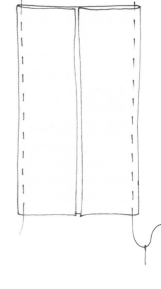

You will need
- Plain fabric (see Calculating fabric, below), pre-washed and dried
- Basic sewing kit, including strong sewing thread
- Prepared indigo vat (see page 8)
- Rubber gloves and apron
- Bowls for soaking and rinsing
- White household vinegar
- Washing detergent
- Iron
- Sewing machine
- Two pieces of ¼ x 1-in. (0.5 x 2.5-cm) wooden batten, the width of your finished shade minus 2 in. (5 cm)
- Hook-and-loop tape
- Small brass rings
- Cord
- Screw eyes
- 1 x 1 in. (2.5 x 2.5 cm) wooden batten
- Drill
- Cleat for the cord

2 Fold over and hem both sides of the fabric, using a double 1-in. (2.5-cm) hem. Turn up a double 2-in. (5-cm) hem along the bottom and stitch close to the fold to form a channel for the lower batten—both ends of the channel need to be open. Check your desired drop again and turn over the top edge to this measurement. Press. Cut a piece of hook-and-loop tape to the width of your shade and stitch the loop (soft) side to the top of the shade.

Calculating Fabric
To calculate how much fabric you need, work out how long and wide you want the finished shade to be; it's up to you whether you hang the shade on the inside or the outside of the window recess. Add 4 in. (10 cm) to both the width and the length, to allow for the hems.

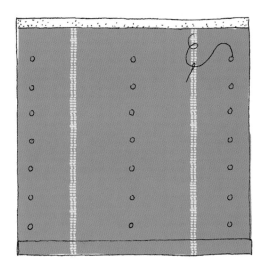

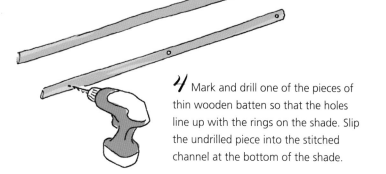

4 Mark and drill one of the pieces of thin wooden batten so that the holes line up with the rings on the shade. Slip the undrilled piece into the stitched channel at the bottom of the shade.

3 In order to work out how many brass rings you need, you will need to decide how many folds you would like in the shade when it is pulled up—they should be evenly spaced and can be anything from 6–10 in. (15–25 cm) apart. Each fold will need three rings—one at each side and one in the center (for very wide shades you may need another line of rings). Pin and stitch the rings in place according to your calculations.

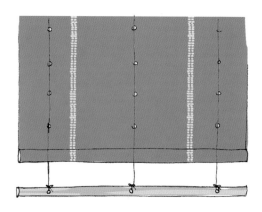

5 Take three pieces of cord and tie them through the holes that you have drilled in the thin wooden batten. Then thread them vertically up through the rings on the shade.

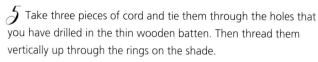

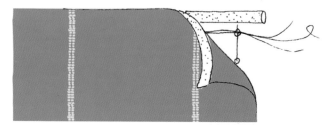

6 Fix the three screw eyes into the underside of the 1 x 1 in. (2.5 x 2.5 cm) wooden batten so that they line up with the rings on the shade. Fix the batten in place on the wall or window frame and then staple the hook (stiff) side of the hook-and-loop tape to the front of the batten. Attach the shade to the batten using the hook-and-loop tape and then pass the cords through the screw eyes. Arrange so that the cords are even, knot firmly, and trim the ends. Fix the cleat to the wall or window frame, and loop the cords around it.

tab-topped *curtains*

Tab-topped curtains with a simple striped pattern decorate a window with style. Dipping the gathered portions first makes the pattern stand out beautifully!

1 Mark with pencil where you would like the stripes. You want them to be evenly spaced, so use a tape measure to work out where they should be, making sure you allow for the hems and the 8-in. (20-cm) strip that you remove for the tabs (see step 4).

You will need

- Two lengths of unbleached calico (see Calculating fabric, below)
- Basic sewing kit, including strong thread
- Cotton webbing tape, 1 in. (2.5 cm) wide and the length of your curtain width, plus 6 in. (15 cm)
- Prepared indigo vat (see page 8)
- Rubber gloves and apron
- Bowls for soaking and rinsing
- White household vinegar
- Washing detergent
- Iron

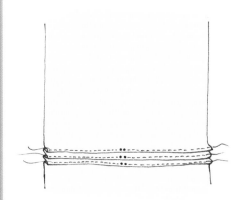

2 For each "stripe" you need to fold and stitch three rows of fabric: start in the center of the middle row and stitch out to the edge of the fabric (this making pulling up the stitches easier), remembering to secure the thread with a firm knot. Then stitch out from the center to the other side. Repeat above and below this first row to create three rows. Fold where marked and stitch along the folds. Carefully pull up all three threads and secure with a knot, first on one side and then the other.

3 Once all the stitching is complete gather up the fabric with the loose ends and secure tightly. Soak, dye and rinse as instructed on page 91, then wash with detergent and dry. When completely dry, iron the dyed fabric.

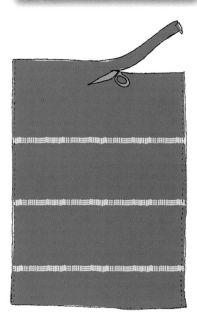

4 Trim the bottom hem edges where they may have frayed during dyeing. Remove a strip 8 in. (20 cm) deep from the top of each dyed curtain and cut each piece into six strips. Fold each tab in half lengthwise, wrong sides together, and machine stitch, taking a ⅜-in. (1-cm) seam allowance. Trim the seam allowance, then press the seam open, centering it in the middle of the tab. Turn the tab right side out.

Calculating Fabric

Measure the required drop of the curtain and add on 13 in. (32.5 cm) for the tabs and bottom hem. Measure the width and add on 4 in (10 cm) for the side hems, plus an extra 50% for fullness (increase this amount if you want a more gathered curtain.) Cut two pieces of fabric to these measurements.

5 Turn under and stitch a double 1-in. (2.5-cm) hem on each side of each curtain. Fold up and stitch a double 2-in. (5-cm) hem along the bottom of each curtain. Fold each tab in half, with the seam on the inside, and place along the top of the curtain, right sides together and with the raw edges level, so that the tabs are pointing downward. Pin, then machine stitch in place, taking a ¾-in. (2-cm) seam allowance.

6 Pin and stitch the dyed webbing tape along the tops of the curtains, covering the ends of the stitched tabs. Leave 1½ in. (4 cm) overhanging at each end—this will be folded in to cover the raw edges.

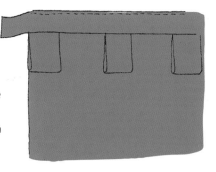

7 Fold the tape overlap in at each end and then fold the tape over to the wrong side of the curtains. Press in place and then pin and machine stitch along the bottom edge of the tape to secure.

Flowers *apron*

*Plain cotton drill aprons are easily found and just as easily dyed.
Using a fresh indigo vat gives a very dark indigo blue, which shows off
the attractive pattern well!*

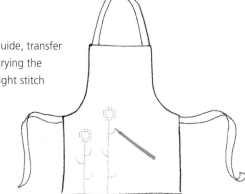

You will need
- Templates on page 109
- Pencil
- Plain cotton drill apron in white, cream, or ecru
- Needle and strong thread
- Prepared indigo vat (see page 8)
- Rubber gloves and apron
- Bowls for soaking and rinsing
- White household vinegar
- Washing detergent
- Iron

1 Using the templates on page 109 as a guide, transfer the flowers onto the apron using a pencil, varying the height of the flowers for a pretty effect. Straight stitch (see page 88) the flower heads and stem, taking note of the direction of the stitches shown on the templates, then fold and stitch (see page 89) where indicated to create leaf shapes.

2 Once all the stitching is complete pull up the free ends to gather the fabric tightly and secure.

3 Soak and dye the apron, following the instructions on page 91.

4 Rinse well, adding white vinegar to the final rinse. Wash in detergent, and allow the apron to dry.

5 Once the apron is completely dry, press gently with an iron.

square *lampshade*

This pattern of overlapping circles is a simple but effective contrast to the square-shaped lampshade.

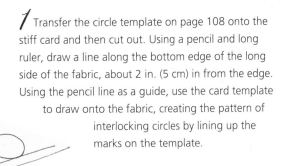

1 Transfer the circle template on page 108 onto the stiff card and then cut out. Using a pencil and long ruler, draw a line along the bottom edge of the long side of the fabric, about 2 in. (5 cm) in from the edge. Using the pencil line as a guide, use the card template to draw onto the fabric, creating the pattern of interlocking circles by lining up the marks on the template.

You will need
- Template on page 108
- Tracing paper
- Pencil and ruler
- Stiff card
- Scissors
- Lampshade kit
- Fabric in one piece, large enough to cover your lampshade (refer to the kit instructions)
- Diagram on page 108
- Needle and strong thread
- Prepared indigo vat (see page 8)
- Rubber gloves and apron
- Bowls for soaking and rinsing
- White household vinegar
- Washing detergent

2 Thread a needle with a length of strong thread. Pinch and stitch along the lines (see page 89), noting the direction of stitching on the diagram on page 108. Only stitch short parts of the pattern each time—you may want to stitch whole circles at a time but it's important to stitch the short curves in pairs to make gathering the fabric easier. Gently pull up the threads in pairs and tie them together.

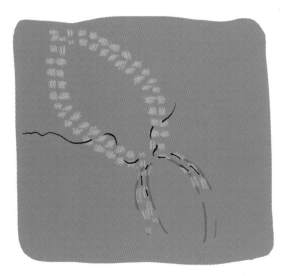

3 Dye and rinse the fabric following the instructions on page 91. Unpick all the stitches only when the fabric is well rinsed: carefully snip away a few stitches and gently pull the fabric apart to remove the stitches. Wash and dry and then press with an iron.

4 Assemble the shade following the instructions included with the kit.

bed *Throw*

If you would like to try out all the different shibori nui techniques at once, this is the perfect project for you. The small squares are easy to handle in the vat, and they combine to create a beautiful patchwork effect.

1 Prepare the 21 squares of fabric, using various stitched shibori patterns (see pages 88–90). Dye the fabric, along with the four pieces of plain cotton, following the instructions on page 91. When dry, iron on the correct setting.

You will need

- 21 squares of linen and/or calico cotton, each measuring 8¾ x 8¾ in. (22 x 22 cm)
- Basic sewing kit
- Iron
- Four pieces of plain cotton, each measuring 52 x 8¾ in. (133 x 22 cm)
- Prepared indigo vat (see page 8)
- Rubber gloves and apron
- Bowls for soaking and rinsing
- White household vinegar
- Washing detergent
- Backing fabric measuring 52 x 52 in. (133 x 133 cm)—I used a brushed cotton sheet to gave a lightly quilted effect
- Sewing machine

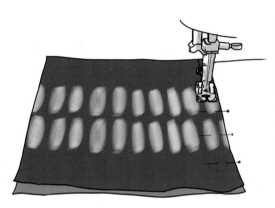

2 Arrange the squares into three strips of seven squares, making sure you alternate the patterns to create a pleasing arrangement. Pin the first two squares right sides together and then use a sewing machine to stich together, taking a ⅝-in. (1.5-cm) seam allowance. Continue until you have seven squares stitched together and then repeat with the other two strips.

3 Press all the seams open with an iron.

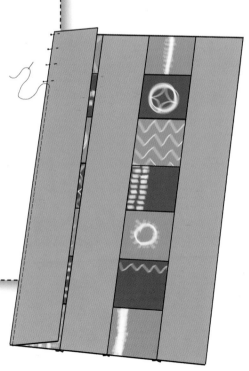

4 Join one long strip of plain dyed fabric to one strip of joined squares by placing them right sides together. Pin and then machine stitch, taking a ⅝-in. (1.5-cm) seam allowance. Add the remaining strips of fabric, alternating the plain and stitched strips as shown in the photograph. Press all the seams open.

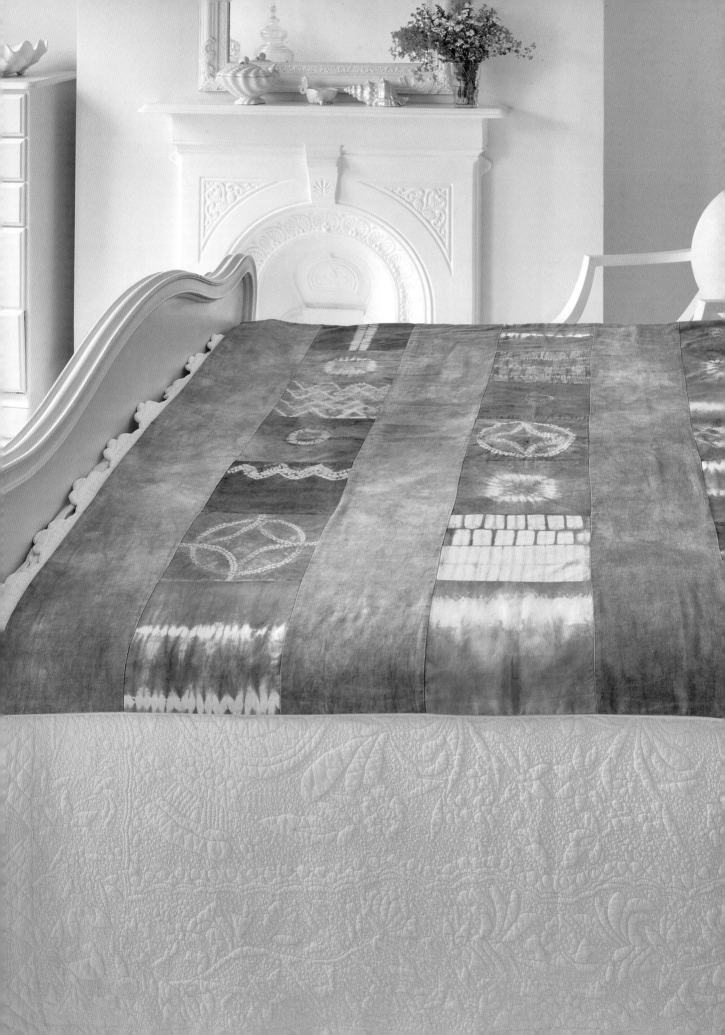

5 With right sides facing, pin the backing fabric to the quilt. Machine stitch all around, taking a ⅝-in. (1.5-cm) seam allowance and leaving a gap about 12 in. (30 cm) long along one side through which the throw can be turned right side out.

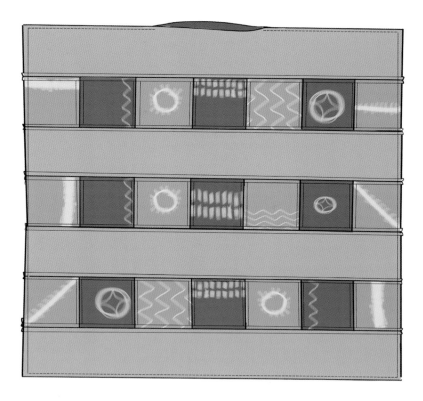

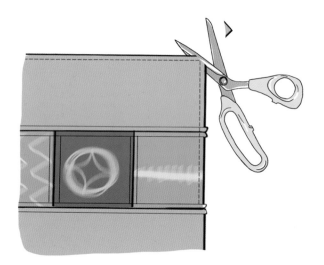

6 Snip across the corners of the seam allowances, being careful not to cut through the stitching—this reduces the amount of fabric allowing the corners to turn out neatly. Turn the quilt out the right way and press round the edge seams with an iron.

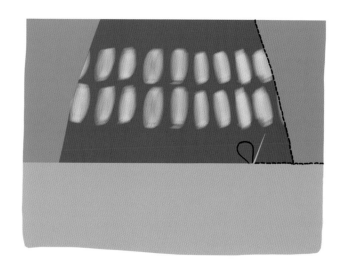

7 Slipstitch the opening closed, then topstitch around some of the squares to hold the two layers of fabric together.

Sewing Techniques

Most of the techniques you will need are described in the project instructions, but there are a few extra bits of information here that will help you get a good finish on your sewing.

Bias binding

Using bias binding to finish hems gives a neat, smooth finish. Bias binding is cut diagonally across the grain of the fabric, which means that it will stretch slightly. There are two ways of doing this, depending on whether the bias binding is to show on only one, or both, sides of the fabric.

For binding to show on one side only:

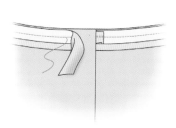

1 Open out one side of the binding and pin it around the edge of the fabric, with the right side of the binding facing the wrong side of the fabric. Stitch together along the crease line, then trim close to the seam.

2 Trim the seam and turn all the binding over to the right side of the fabric.

3 Pin the folded edge of the binding to the right side of the fabric, and topstitch in place.

For binding to show on both sides:

1 Fold the binding in half lengthwise, and fit it over the edge of the fabric. Pin in place

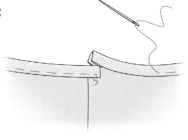

2 Stitch through the binding and the fabric, either by hand or with a machine.

3 Where the binding overlaps, trim away the binding underneath to about ½ in. (12 mm), fold under the end of the other piece of binding by about ½ in. (12 mm), and lay it over, before stitching through all layers.

Seam binding tape

Use seam binding tape to create neat straight edges, without bulky hems. The technique is the same for applying heading tape to curtains.

1 Fold the fabric over once by about ½ in. (1 cm) and press with an iron.

2 Cover the raw edge of the fabric with the seam binding tape and pin in place, just below the fold line, before topstitching along each side of the tape.

Piping

Piping is a great way to give a neat finish to pillow (cushion) seams and it's easier than it looks! You will need to use a zipper or piping foot on your machine.

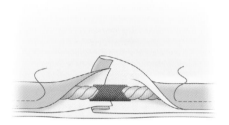

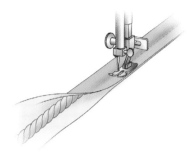

1 Cut 2 in. (5 cm) wide strips across the bias of the fabric (diagonally). Cutting on the bias means that the fabric will stretch slightly around curves and you won't get wrinkles forming.

2 Fit the zipper or piping foot on to your machine.

3 To cover the cord, place the piping cord down the center of the bias strip on the wrong side. Bring the long edges of the bias strip together around the cord and stitch down the length close to the cord, using the side of the foot as a guide.

4 If the ends of the cord need to be joined, unpick the machine stitching on the piping for about 2 in. (5 cm) at each end, and fold back the bias strip. Trim each end of the piping so that the ends of the cord will butt up against one another, then bind the ends together with thread. Turn under ¼ in. (6 mm) at one end of the bias strip and slip this over the raw end. Baste (tack) in place close to the cord.

Trimming seam allowances

When sewing sharp-angled corners or circles, you will need to trim the seams before pressing them open, to get a neat finish.

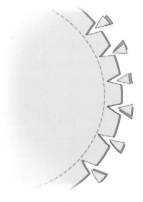

To create a sharp, neat angle, cut across the corner of the seam allowances as shown, close to the stitching, but making sure that you do not cut through the actual stitching. When turning your seam to the right side, use a pair of small, pointed scissors or a knitting needle to carefully push out the point, making sure that you do not push too hard and form a hole.

Notching or clipping curved seams

Notches are small wedges of fabric cut from the seam allowances of outward curves, as shown here, to allow them to lie smooth and flat. On inward curves you only need to clip into the seam allowances so that the edges will spread out and lie flat. Use a small pair of sharp, pointed scissors, to notch or clip at regular intervals, taking care to cut close to but not through the stitches.

Stitches

There are a few stitches used in the projects, to provide a neat seam or a decorative finish.

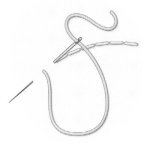

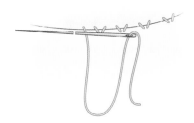

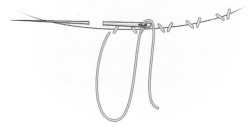

Backstitch

Bring the needle up through the fabric and take a short backward stitch on the stitching line. Bring the needle through again a stitch-length in front of the first stitch. Take the needle back down where it first came through, and repeat along the stitching line.

Slipstitch

Slipstitch is nearly invisible and is used to sew up a gap in a seam from the right side of the fabric

Working from right to left, bring the needle through one folded edge of fabric, slip the needle through the fold of the opposite edge for about ¼ in. (6 mm), and draw the needle and thread through. Continue in this way to join both edges.

Templates

These templates are all reproduced at full size.

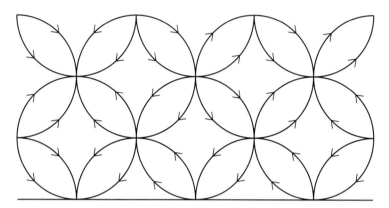

Lampshade page 101:
arrows show direction of stitching for overlaid circles

Lampshade page 101
Circle

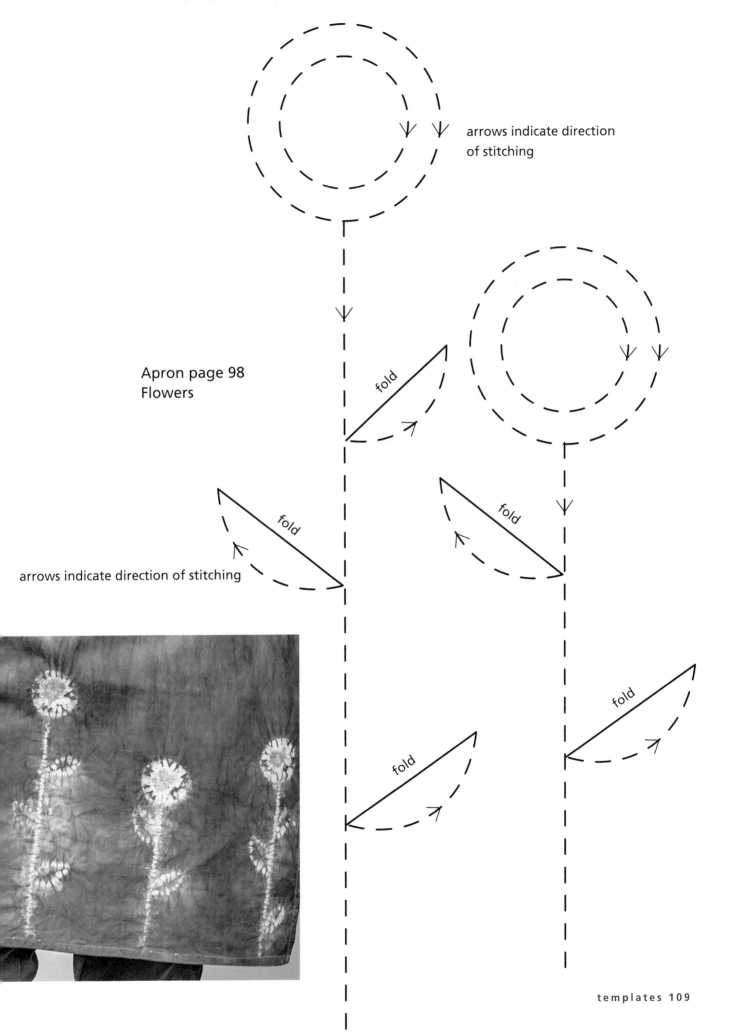

arrows indicate direction
of stitching

Apron page 98
Flowers

fold

fold

fold

arrows indicate direction of stitching

fold

fold

fold

suppliers

US

The Woolery
315 St Clair St Street
Frankfort
KY 40601
Tel: 800 441 9665
www.woolery.com

Dharma Trading Co.
1604 Fourth Street
San Rafael
CA 94901
Tel: 800 542 5227
www.dharmatrading.com

General craft supplies:

Jo-Ann Fabric and Craft Stores
Store finder on website.
www.joann.com

Michaels
Store finder on website.
www.michaels.com

UK

Halfpenny Home
The Dovecote at Alder Carr Farm
Creeting St Mary
IP6 8LX
Tel: 01449 721123
www.halfpennyhome.co.uk
www.halfpennyhome.blogspot.com
For dyeing workshops, stitching tuition,
notions, and general craft supplies, including
undyed textiles.

Sewing classes can be found all over the
place. I run many at Halfpenny Home,
but I can also recommend those run at
www.felixstowesewingschool.co.uk by
Amanda Bowden

George Weil (Fibrecrafts)
Old Portsmouth Road
Peasmarch
Guildford GU3 1LZ
Tel: 01483 565800
www.georgeweil.com
For indigo dye, spectralite, and soda ash.

General craft supplies:

Hobbycraft
Store finder on website.
www.hobbycraft.co.uk

John Lewis
Store finder on website.
www.johnlewis.com

index

acknowledgments

Thanks to my family and friends who have helped enormously during the production of this book, particularly Jonathan Oxborrow for his patience, for driving a car full of finished projects to London on his day off, and for not minding my blue hands when my rubber gloves developed a hole.

Thank you especially to my parents for their support, for teaching me to have no fear, to "always try something or you'll always wonder what might have happened," and for stepping in when I need extra help.

Thanks also to my "craft consultants" Lynne Pratt and Jenny Tidman for helping me decide on projects, Samantha Hayes for getting me into natural dyes all those years ago—I'll never forgive you!—and Christina Hamilton for generously letting me use her Heart Garland pattern. Thanks to Nigel and Julie "Sweetpea" Smith for finding me buckets, bowls, jugs, and pans along with many other requests, making me believe that they can find absolutely anything, and to Paddy Peters and Helen Brown for inspiring me with their beautiful pottery and love of nature.

A special thank you must go to all at Alder Carr Farm, who have been so friendly and helpful while we were moving the shop to its present location in an old windmill on the farm. Nick and Joan Hardingham kindly allowed us to use the farm for some of the photography—we couldn't ask for a prettier backdrop.

Thank you to everyone at CICO Books, who have all worked so hard to make this beautiful book! Particularly Penny Craig, Sally Powell, and Gillian Haslam who have all been so patient and supportive. Thank you to Gavin Kingcome for his stunning photography, professionalism, and dedication. One day we'll stop laughing about him falling in the pond... and finally, thank you to Cindy Richards, who saw the beauty of shibori, and how it could be used to decorate our homes.